the
geometry
of
being
Black.

Copyright © 2018 by Ogorchukwu.
All rights reserved.
ISBN 10: 1719276005
ISBN-13: 978-1719276009

for me,
for you,
for us –
the community.

in this life,
you will receive
and internalize
anti-Blackness.
but this life
will also grant you
the breath to
unlearn it,
resist it,
and love your Blackness
again.

themes.

receiving — 11

internalizing — 43

unlearning — 79

loving — 115

resisting — 145

a story
that begins with disempowerment,
does not need
to end there.

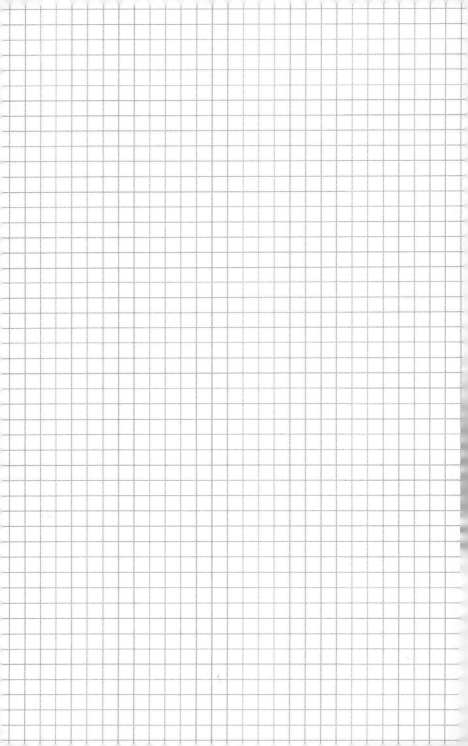

receiving.

ogorchukwu

she recounts the day
she gave birth to twins—
how one was pulled
from her arms,
and bound by the slave trade,
how the other remained
in her arms
but was bound by colonization.
she tells me,
"this is what it means to be
separated at birth."

–africans and african americans

the geometry of being Black

the way the earth
recoils
as you thrust
for resources
she did not
say
you could take.
did you not learn
that even continents
must consent?

ogorchukwu

to rupture
our bodies,
our people,
our land.
to build
homes
on our
dismemberment.

–settler

back then
our motherland wailed
as we were
ripped from her womb.
today,
she whimpers
as we struggle
to recall
her scent,
her touch,
her.

ogorchukwu

how many tongues
were swallowed,
how many voices
were lost,
in the smothering
of our people?

the geometry of being Black

the histories
written into our skin,
the lifelines
threaded into our palms,
erased
and unraveled.

ogorchukwu

the fear of having to
birth Blackness
in a world that is
afraid of the dark.

the geometry of being Black

the way capitalism
and racism
make love every night
and wreak havoc every morning—
sell your child a toy gun
one day
and murder them for playing with it
the next.

–november 22, 2014

ogorchukwu

Black women do not
plant seeds
and watch them sprout,
only for them to be ripped
from the soil
by those who find them
disposable.

the geometry of being Black

Black boys bleed red.

–human

ogorchukwu

a system
that plants children in soil
riddled with weeds
and then uproots them
for not flourishing.

–mass incarceration

the geometry of being Black

i was taught that love
had no boundaries,
and watched
my people
be barred from it.

ogorchukwu

i am not sure what frightens me more—
the type of racism that you can see,
which fearlessly floods the streets,
or the type of racism that hides,
which quietly trickles down the pipes.

i know cities where our blood pumps lead.

–flint

the geometry of being Black

some days,
our bodies feel
the silent aches.
some days,
our throats trap
the silent cries.
some days,
we carry the pain
of those
who came before us.

–epigenetics

how dare you
paint
a skin that holds so much warmth,
cold.

the geometry of being Black

he asked me
why the innocence
of a Black man
deserved less protection
than the violence
of a white man.

i could not answer.

all the women
whose
necks you held
as you strummed
their bodies
for songs that were not
yours
to play.

–daniel holtzclaw's guitar

"cover up," he says,
as if
that will stop
those men
from treating
the region
between my thighs
as their
canal.

–middle passage

ogorchukwu

we were
told that the world
couldn't hold our tears.
our bodies were turned
into droughts,
our organs
into famines.

–unlearning how to water ourselves

even as she cries,
her tears feed a soil
she never asked
to be planted on.

–always taking

ogorchukwu

too many Black boys
being taught
that their strength
comes from their horsepower
and not their brainpower.

–matter over mind.

the women
were taught that
their value was based on
their ability to birth.

the men
were taught that
their value was based on
their ability to exert.

somewhere along the line,
this world began to believe
that all we had to offer
was labor.

ogorchukwu

pick at my hair
like it is
a field of cotton.
pick at my hair
like i do not
deserve agency
here
either.

the geometry of being Black

erasure
is violent.
erasure
in books,
in films,
in toys,
in lesson plans,
will teach our children
that their bodies do not
deserve
to take up space,
do not deserve
to exist.

–un. representation

the way
Blackness is
exploited,
collected,
examined,
and presented.
the way
Blackness is
reduced to artifacts
in museums.
something about
your curation
feels bloody.

the geometry of being Black

dehumanization.

ogorchukwu

how to revive
a people
who have been
torn,
ground,
and swallowed—
how to revive
what has passed
through the body
of oppression.

–digestion

the geometry of being Black

how many times
have we been told
to *get over it?*

how many times
have we been told
this hate against our skin
is *our own doing?*

–gaslight

ogorchukwu

the earth still carries
my broken pieces.
i feel them everywhere
i go.

–residue

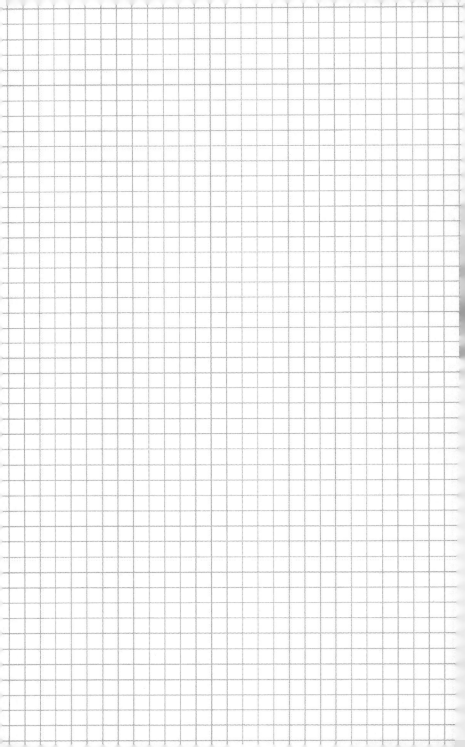

internalizing.

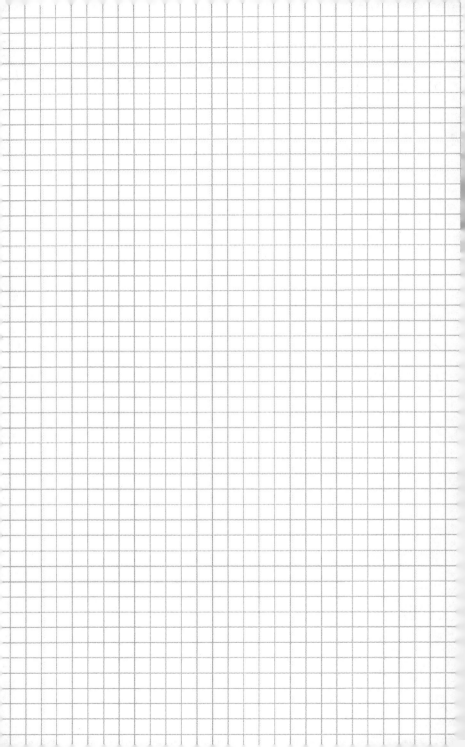

many of us have spent lifetimes
hearing,
reading,
visualizing,
and experiencing
this disdain against our skin.

–the four types of learning

the geometry of being Black

i have
redecorated,
rearranged,
redusted,
made homes out of my skin
more times than
i can count.
but on some days,
it could not feel
more
unwelcoming.

ogorchukwu

he tells me
he no longer looks
at mirrors.
he is tired of seeing the word
worthless,
flooding from
his skin.
i wish there
were levees
for this type of hate.

–self

they say that what you ingest while
pregnant will impact your child.
my mother swallowed her language,
and i was born with no tongue.
where is my mother's tongue?

–immigrant

it is human instinct
to flee from what does not feel safe.
perhaps
this is why
many of us flee
from this skin.

–fight or flight

the geometry of being Black

you swear
that there are pathogens
in the cells,
tissues,
and fluids
layered into your skin—
that your Blackness
is something
that needs to be cured.

–hypochondriac

the irony is that
the system which tells us
to bury our Blackness
under covers—
will not comfort us.

–respectability politics

the geometry of being Black

acid reflux
when i swallow my Blackness.
there is a bitterness
that comes
with devouring oneself.

–Black face, white space

ogorchukwu

you fall to your knees,
clasp your hands,
and rebuke your skin.
as if divinity itself
does not breathe in all that Black
that cocoons your bones.

—a morning prayer

the geometry of being Black

it hurts to know
that when racism
gave birth to colorism,
we cradled it
like it was
our own.

too /to͞o/: to an excessive degree.

black /blak/: having dark pigmentation of the skin.

these are two distinct words
in the dictionary.
only we have the power
to place them
side by side.

–too Black

the geometry of being Black

some nights i weep
for all those
who were made
to swallow
their sun.

–bleach

all those years we spent
in front of the mirror
trying to overcome
our Blackness
with whiteness.
all those years we spent
in front of the mirror
trying to excuse the
colonization taking place
within our bodies.

the geometry of being Black

the first time my hair was relaxed, i was not old enough to question it, to question why we had to degrade my scalp, why we had to insult my hair follicles, why we had to humiliate my coils, why my beauty was tied to conditioning the Blackness out of me.

–conditioned roots

there is something
so tragic
about believing
that hair is not good enough,
because it is not *white enough*.

there is something
so tragic
about believing
that beauty,
cannot be found in Blackness.

–good hair

the geometry of being Black

when the hurt
comes from your own
self.
family.
community.
when the hurt
feels autoimmune.

ogorchukwu

how to love your own kin
when you've been taught
to despise your own skin.

the geometry of being Black

i never fit your description of a daytime lover. to you, my body was only good for loving past 2 a.m., when it was too dark for you to see your reflection through my eyes and accept that your skin was just as Black as mine.

—"i don't date Black girls"

ogorchukwu

my heart shatters for every single
Black girl who has been told
that her deep skin tone
is not worthy of a deep love,
every single Black girl
who has been made to hear
the teachings of the oppressor
from her own community.

the geometry of being Black

you tell me i am beautiful
and then proceed to ask me
if i am fully Black,
as if i am not the product
of the sun and the moon
themselves,
as if the brown in my skin
is not the result of the warmth
of a thousand suns,
as if the glow in my skin
is not the reflection
of a thousand moons.
honey,
i was conceived by Blackness.
give credit where it is due.

ogorchukwu

the subtle
and unsubtle ways
you teach
your daughters
to despise their skin,
teaches
their brothers
to despise it too.

–homeschooling

the geometry of being Black

some of us spend
lifetimes
trying to weed out racism
while our garden gloves
are soiled
with colorism.
some of us spend
lifetimes
trying to remove a stain
with dirt.

ogorchukwu

our people
have been abused
for so many lifetimes,
some of us have grown to find
safety in threats,
caresses in fists,
and warmth in isolation.

the geometry of being Black

you call him a coward
for loving
another Black boy,
as if loving
someone like himself,
in a world that tells him
to despise
someone like himself,
is not the single
most
revolutionary act.

ogorchukwu

to degrade
the types of Black
that are queer,
that are not bound
by your definition
of what Black
should be–
is a form of
anti–Blackness.

the geometry of being Black

to be taught that power
can only be derived
from abuse.

–a colonial lesson plan

ogorchukwu

think of the
soul drought
you create
when you forbid your son
from crying.

the geometry of being Black

you drink patriarchy
like milk.
you let it ferment your bones,
thinking it makes you strong.
but i watch your bones fracture,
i watch your bones dissolve.
i hope you come to learn
that true power
is not built
by dominating
those around you.

ogorchukwu

last night we cried
about the way history
taught us that
consent
does not apply to Black women.
about the way we have
normalized
the robbery of
the Black woman's
body.

—us too

the geometry of being Black

she tells me
she has adapted thorns
to protect herself
from those
who only wish to
shear her,
pluck her,
and peel away her petals.
that
being an *angry Black woman*
is about self-preservation.

ogorchukwu

why do we expect Black women
to dissect their liberation?
to place their Blackness
before their womanhood
or their womanhood
before their Blackness?
Black women
are the epitome of what happens
when two
worlds collide.
take us whole
or not at all.

–at the intersection

the geometry of being Black

it is not this skin
you despise.
it is the way
this skin
is treated.

–pinpoint

receiving pain
does not mean you have to
give pain.
certain things
need not be
passed on.

–generational trauma

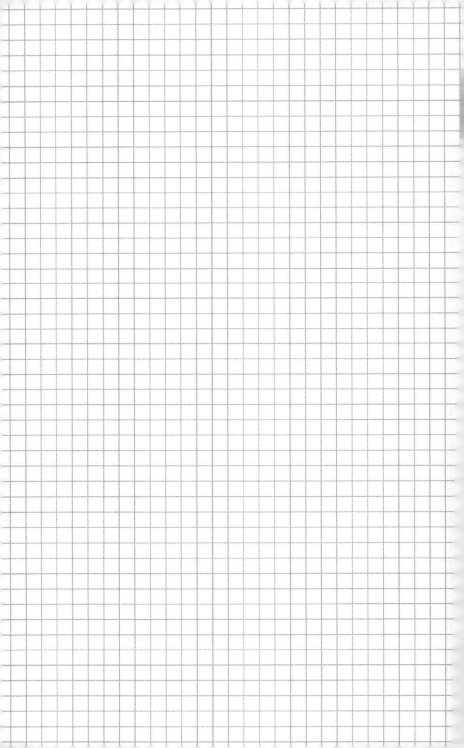

unlearning.

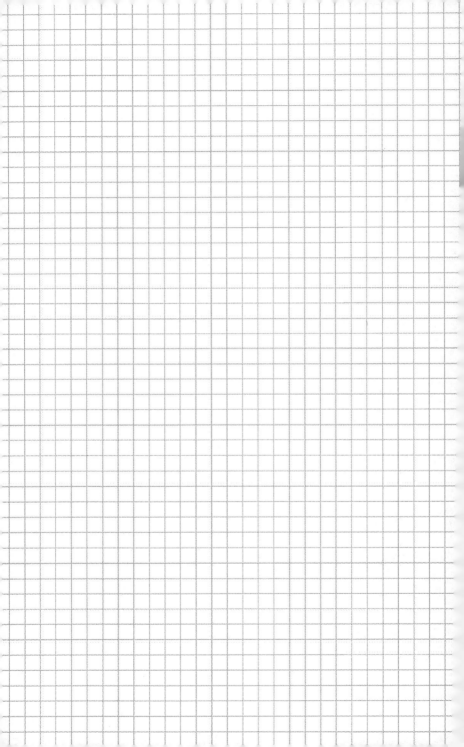

ogorchukwu

sometimes unlearning
self-hate
will feel like
resetting bones
that have been dislocated
for far too long.

the geometry of being Black

many of those
who came before us
were taught
to expect less love,
to expect lest respect,
to expect less kindness.
challenge yourself
to dislocate the cycle—
to no longer
seek comfort
in shortage.

self-love
is lining your skin
with seeds of love.
it is nourishing
these seeds.
it is enduring
the growing pains
as they bloom.
self-love is labor,
but you will reap
the fruits.

the geometry of being Black

believe me when i tell you
that you are whole,
that you do not deserve
to be loved in pieces.

ogorchukwu

as a child, i was always afraid to show my wounds to my mother. i knew that she would bring out the rubbing alcohol and that as soon as it made contact with my skin, it would sting. i began to associate healing with pain, and so i tried my best to avoid it. later on in life, i learned that the initial sting is vital. wounds cannot heal if you do not tend to them. they only worsen, becoming more polluted, more pervasive.

confront your hurt—
revel in the initial pain.
healing will come soon enough.

the geometry of being Black

i sat in a warm bath filled with
chamomile
and watched the hate
swell down.
this
is how my body made room
for love.

–anti-inflammatory

ogorchukwu

teach your children
that their skin is not soil
to be trampled on
but a sanctuary
that houses flowers.

–flowerbeds

the geometry of being Black

there are temples
in your Blackness.
your body
is a dwelling place.
do not let the world
trick you into thinking
that your Blackness
houses tombs,
that your body is
a burial ground.

ogorchukwu

i pray for steady hands
to mold tenderness
back into the bodies
that have been
hardened
by the callous knuckles
of oppression.

–pottery class

the geometry of being Black

this healing
feels more like salt
than like honey,
but my father tells me
salt
can be just as powerful.

–disinfectant

ogorchukwu

breakdown
to
breakthrough.

the geometry of being Black

if they tell you
that all you are
is a body,
if they tell you
that you lack
a mind that races
and a soul that aches,
teach yourself to breathe—
to exhale all
that defies your being,
to inhale all
that supports your humanity.

ogorchukwu

you are a warrior,
but you were not gifted
with all of this strength
to be at war
with yourself.

the geometry of being Black

nourish your sons.
plant seeds of tenderness
in their skin
so that they may learn
to tend to roses
and not wince
at the touch of petals.

–healthy masculinity

it is not in softness
that we break,
but in hardness.

the geometry of being Black

sometimes when you are surrounded by brokenness, all you know is shattered pieces that cut your hands, scarred your hands, over and over, until they hardened. and now in their hardness, they damage everything they hold. everything close to your heart. just know that it's okay to put the things you love down, so that you may learn to soften your hands. so that you may learn to love without breaking.

ogorchukwu

when your tears overflow,
when they seep into your
rigid skin,
know they are not here
to drown you
but to nurture your being
back to tenderness.
see those flowers blooming
in your skin?

the geometry of being Black

do not let
the hate
embrace you.
do not let
it mold
to fit to your body.
do not let it
remember
you.

–memory foam

ogorchukwu

imagine
owning your Blackness
the way society
tries to.

the geometry of being Black

believe in your innocence.

ogorchukwu

i will spend a lifetime
uprooting the hate
planted in my skin
so that my children
may spend eternities
growing love in theirs.

–gardening

the geometry of being Black

learning to embrace
the roses
rooted in dark skin
as much as you embrace
the roses
rooted in light skin,
is how you begin to weed out
the life
that upholds hate
as the primary aesthetic.

know that there is no sin
in birthing color.
there is, however,
an artistic virtue
in a womb
that spends its months painting.

–masterpiece of color

the geometry of being Black

do not look at yourself
through society's mirror.
this mirror
does not belong to you.

–false reflections

ogorchukwu

Black women are resilient,
but this does not mean
that we do not feel
the weight of pain.
this does not mean
that our shoulders do not
bend, fracture, or break.
it is our tears that bait floods,
our cries that entice hurricanes,
our sobs that provoke tsunamis.
it is our pain
that aches the earth.
do you feel it?

the geometry of being Black

be a gatekeeper
for your young ones.
guard them from the floods
of animosity that will
try to drown them
before they can
anchor themselves.

learn to educate with petals
instead of pebbles.
sometimes tender love
is a better teacher
than tough love.

erupt. release the magma brewing under your skin. spew out all the lava, the ashes, and the rocks circulating your veins. the beauty of volcanic eruptions is that their residue contains minerals that rebuild the surrounding soil. so erupt. then rebuild.

ogorchukwu

there is always space
to invest in the *quality*
of the community.

—accountability

the geometry of being Black

it is not wrong
to feel nostalgic about yourself.
you are right
to question why
you ever left yourself
in the first place.

–homesick

ogorchukwu

i am teaching myself
how to be
the sea.
when you peel away
a layer of sea,
you find more of it.
and if you break
the sea into streams,
it simply returns
to itself.

–full

the geometry of being Black

unlearning is uprooting,
and it is painful,
so be tender with yourself.
water your soil,
massage your layers,
allow the roots to loosen
before you sever them.

still,
you are more
than
your pain.

loving.

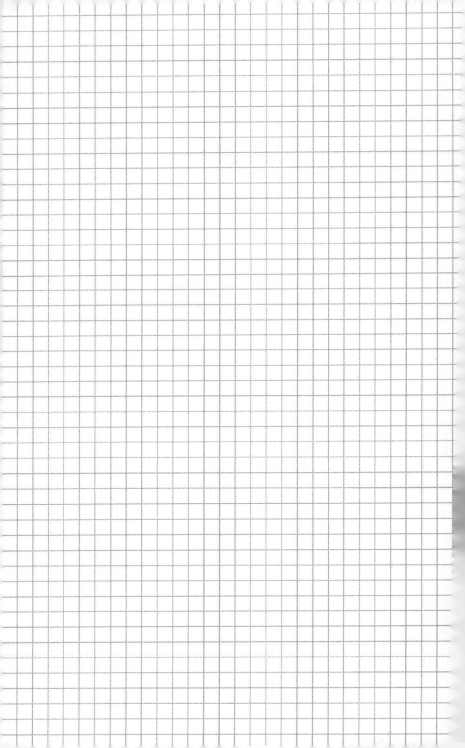

ogorchukwu

come here.
let me love up on that skin they hate so much.

–for the love of Blackness

the geometry of being Black

my mother gave birth to a poem
the color of the earth,
and i wear the words
so beautifully.

—skin

there's something about the way
your mahogany skin
gleams under the sunlight
and glows under the moonlight.

—the sun will not harm you by day, nor the moon by night. Psalm 121:6.

the geometry of being Black

to my unborn,
i promise to line my placenta
with enough gentleness
to dull any hardness
you experience in this world.

–the fetal/maternal exchange

ogorchukwu

you've got eternities in your Blackness.

−space

the geometry of being Black

how you embrace
your skin
is how you guide your children
to embrace theirs.
let there be
a lesson in your self-love.

ogorchukwu

in our younger years,
we would sit in tree houses
and share folktales.
in one tale,
the sun made a vow
to never leave our ancestors.
something about
the brown in our skin
tells me this vow
has never be broken.

the geometry of being Black

my grandmother tells me
that patience
is kneading love into skin
that has been neglected
for lifetimes.

there is something about the way
yellow cloth cocoons Black skin,
like the sun freed some of its rays
and morphed them into something
that would remind us of the way
it loved us into warmth.

the geometry of being Black

your hair
can only be described
as billions of stars
held together
by a gravitational force.
there is nothing
more cosmic than coils
that form
galaxies.

–afro

ogorchukwu

its hurts to think
i ever turned these defiant curls
into weeping willows.
but i have learned to love
the notes,
the pitches,
and the rhythm,
flowing in these curls—
to move with the resistance song
my ancestors blessed me with.

–a hymn

the geometry of being Black

i find rivers
in every crease
in your lips.
i cannot think
of anything more
intuitive
than features that flow.

–full lips

ogorchukwu

that chestnut
that olive
that ivory
that charcoal
that taupe
that ebony
that coffee
that copper
that mahogany
that almond
that Black
is a community of endless palettes.
each color
just as beautiful as the next.

the geometry of being Black

cultivate your children
with love.
show them that
goodness
breathes in this skin,
in this community,
in this Blackness.

ogorchukwu

love
has washed
wars
out of me.

the geometry of being Black

you are predestined
for greatness.
it was written into your story
long before you arrived.
learn to speak power
into your soul,
to embolden
the magic flowing
within you.

–manifestation

ogorchukwu

unfold your skin—
drown yourself
in the love letters
that God pleated
into your complexion.

the geometry of being Black

give yourself permission
to weep,
mourn,
laugh,
and love.

–birthright

more Black joy.

the geometry of being Black

we used to think we were
note–less music sheets.
but we heard the muffled melodies
in each other
and wrote rhythms of love
back into each other.
there is a quiet blessing,
in being able to remember
this song.

–Black love

ogorchukwu

when two black souls fuse,
know that they have
traveled light years
to meet each other
in this space,
in this time.

seeds of love tumbled
out of our lips
when we kissed,
out of our hands
when we touched,
planting themselves
firmly into us.
and now every time
we see sprouts
in our skin,
we are reminded
that love
breathes here.

ogorchukwu

love
has enough room
to house any
type
of Black.

—spectrum

the geometry of being Black

love belongs to you too.

rub love into me.
i hear its molecules
are so minute,
and so potent,
that when applied
to the skin,
they are able to travel from
the epidermis,
to the dermis,
past the capillaries,
into the bloodstream.

–essential oil

the geometry of being Black

let us be a village
whose baptisms
are about being bathed in love,
whose oaths
are about committing to loving,
whose rites of passage
are about working love into each other.

–ritual

ogorchukwu

justice
has always been about love.

resisting.

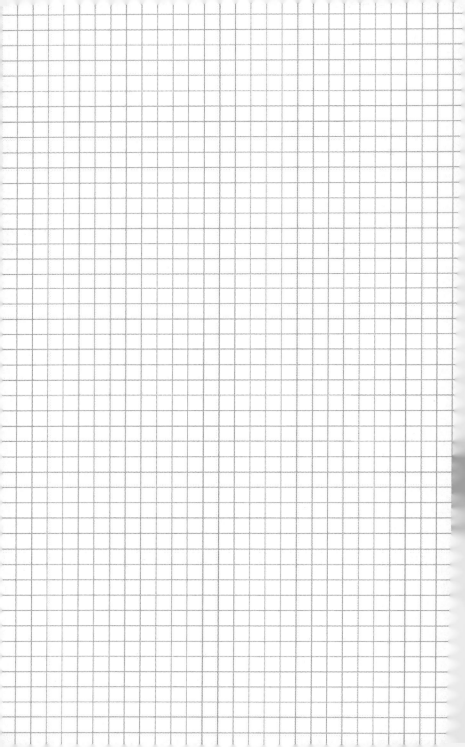

ogorchukwu

the way we turn
agony
into
art.

–alchemy

the geometry of being Black

i feel the warriors in my body
drumming at the walls
of my throat.
each vibration is slowly awakening
the voice
that my body hid in fear.

the revolution
will look like
water
seeking steadiness
after being
displaced.

–tsunami

the geometry of being Black

i recall when
you set me on fire,
hoping that i would
turn to ash,
but i used the fuel
to sustain myself—
i used the fuel
and became light.
how careless of you
to forget
that fires are,
and always have been,
self-perpetuating.

resilience clings to your bones.

—skin deep

the geometry of being Black

when you were taken
from this planet
and lifted into the ethers,
we flooded the streets
the way stardust
floods the sky,
after a supernova has ruptured.

–dear trayvon

maybe it is because
we are brown
that our bodies
are habitually used
as a terrain for war.
maybe it is because
we are women
that our bodies
face a violence excused
as a tragedy of war.
maybe it is because
we are both,
that we are resilient.

–women of color

the geometry of being Black

we will march
until dark
is equal
to light.

—equinox

ogorchukwu

my body pumps the spilt
blood of my ancestors.
my mind feeds off of the resources
stolen from my people's land.
i speak with the caliber of the bullets
used in killing my kinfolk.
all that has been taken from me
has returned to me in a new form.

–reincarnate

the geometry of being Black

you are the one who ate my continent.
do not ask me why
your lips have swelled,
your skin has reddened,
your throat has tightened,
and your stomach is cramping.
perhaps
you should not eat things
that do not belong
to you.

–allergy

ogorchukwu

our mothers
sat in a circle
and drank
wisdom,
knowledge,
and power
as we brewed in their wombs.
this
is how they armed us.

–elixir

the remedy,
for intergenerational trauma
is intergenerational therapy.

—reparations

ogorchukwu

learn to question.

the geometry of being Black

breathe.
there is a silent
resistance
in your presence.

to my Black children,

if they mock
the melanin in your skin,
tell them your skin
glows that much brighter
because the sun
kisses you that much harder.

and if they ridicule
the resilience of your hair,
tell them your hair
defies gravity
because you are not
subject to the principle of the earth.

the geometry of being Black

Black bodies are not disposable.
Black bodies are not disposable.
Black bodies are not disposable.
Black bodies are not disposable.
Black bodies are not disposable.
Black bodies are not disposable.
Black bodies are not disposable.
Black bodies are not disposable.
Black bodies are not disposable.
Black bodies are not disposable.
Black bodies are not disposable.
Black bodies are not disposable.
Black bodies are not disposable.
Black bodies are not disposable.
Black bodies are not disposable.
Black bodies are not disposable.
Black bodies are not disposable.
Black bodies are not disposable.
Black bodies are not disposable.

ogorchukwu

promise me
you will protect
Black women.

−your sister's keeper

the geometry of being Black

i had a dream
that the language of submission
is one we no longer understood.
we no longer
whimpered
and cowered
at your command.
our spines learned to slope,
and our throats learned to growl.

ogorchukwu

break my body
in two
and watch it
build continents.

–tectonic plates

the geometry of being Black

your resistance
can be a stream
or a river.
just make sure it flows.
this is how a movement
is birthed.

ogorchukwu

to my Black sons,

whoever taught you that
strength comes from
swallowing your tears
has never seen the force
of an undammed river.

–cry

the geometry of being Black

all the languages
you made us eat
are foaming
at our lips.
all the languages
you made us bury
are unearthing
themselves.
this upheaval
will have you answering to
every tongue
you made us swallow.

ogorchukwu

take up space.

the geometry of being Black

my mother recounts the story
of how her father was born still,
how his mother placed him
under a tree as she prepared
for his burial,
how he was bitten by bees
and began to squeal.
she tells me,
"resistance swims in your blood."

–igbokwenu

we will line our wombs
with seeds of history
and birth children
with minds that bloom
libraries filled with
truth
and consciousness.

the geometry of being Black

i will never
stop eating.
these books
fill my mouth
with the words
to fight oppression.

–well fed

ogorchukwu

willpower
has been fused
into your muscles.
impenetrability
has been layered
into your skin.
you, my love,
are the vessel
of your ancestors.

travel wisely.

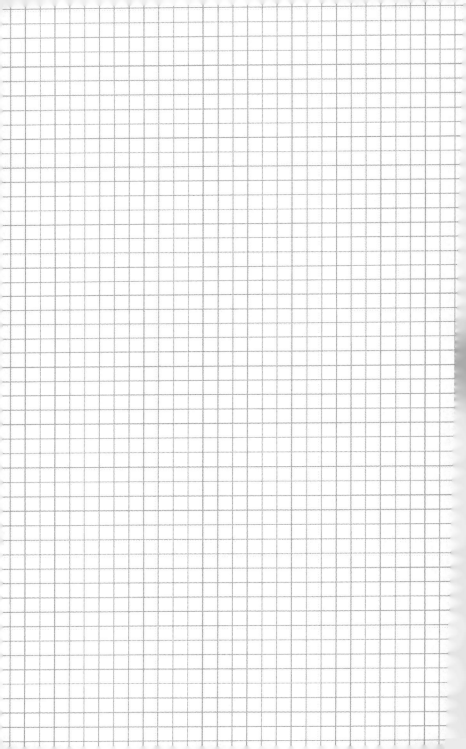

i am a Nigerian American multidisciplinary artist.
my mind operates in words, images, and designs.
my heart beats in justice.
my mission in life is to create art that
whispers,
speaks,
and howls
to the communities
that are often overlooked.

breathe with me on instragram: @ogorchukwuu

some days,
my ancestors
write through me.

—messenger

Made in the USA
San Bernardino, CA
08 June 2020